ANG KWENTO NG MGA NUMERO

THE NUMBER STORY

SMALL BOOK ONE

ENGLISH - TAGALOG

Numbers Teach Children Their Number Names

written and illustrated by

MISS ANNA

Early Reader Edition of *The Number Story 1*
Bronze Medal Winner, 2016 Wishing Shelf Book Award

Library of Congress Control Number: 2018902040

Names: Miss Anna, author.
Title: Number story : numbers teach children their number names / Miss Anna.
Description: Portland, OR: Lumpy Publishing, 2018.
Identifiers: ISBN 978-1-945977-25-1 | LCCN 2018902040
Summary: The pictures and rhymes present stories which introduce numbers 0-10.
Subjects: LCSH Numeration—English--Tagalog--Pictorial works--Juvenile literature. | BISAC JUVENILE NONFICTION /
Languages: English--Tagalog
Classification: LCC QA141.3 .M57 2018 | DDC 513—dc23

Publisher: Lumpy Publishing
Website: www.missannabooks.com
Email: missanna@missannabooks.com

Paperback: ISBN 978-1-945977-25-1
Printed in the U.S.A.   1 3 5 7 9 10 8 6 4 2

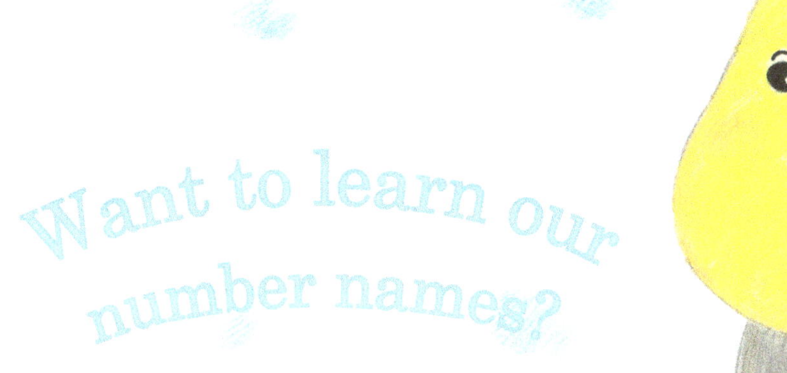

Nais mo bang matutunan ang mga pangalan ng bawat numero?

It is very easy and a lot of fun!

Ito ay napakadali at masayang matutunan!

Say-along our little jingle

Halina't awitin natin ang munting kwento!

starting from Number One!

Ating umpisahan sa Numero Isa!

1

ONE   looks like my one finger.

ISA

ay tulad ng kong daliri.

ONE!
ISA!

2

TWO trails a tail.

DALAWA

samusunod sa buntot.

A TAIL! ISANG BUNTOT!

3

THREE has bumps.

TATLO

ay may babag.

BUMPY!

MABABAG!

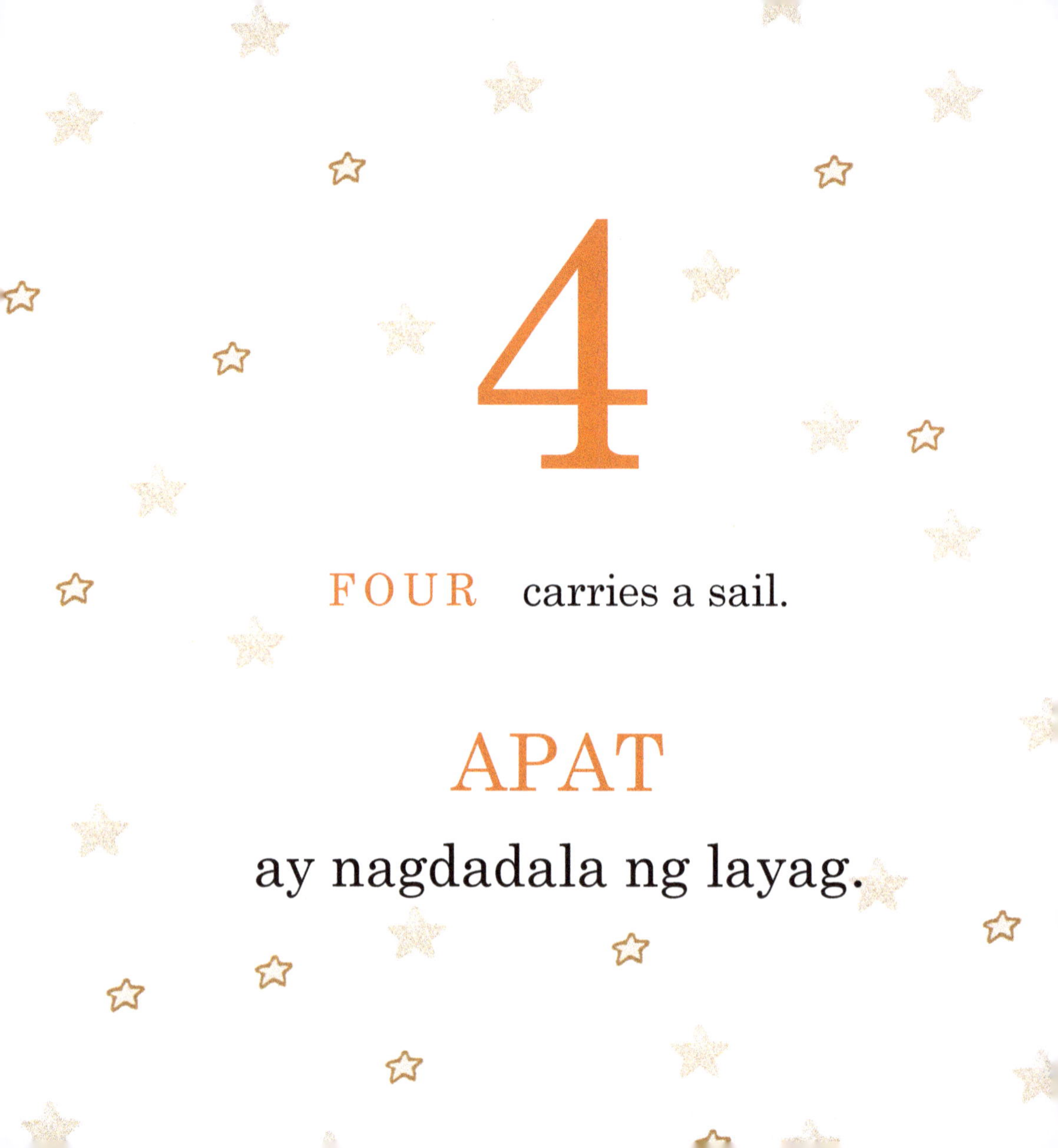

4

FOUR carries a sail.

APAT

ay nagdadala ng layag.

4
A SAIL!
ISANG LAYAG!

5

FIVE   is a racing track.

LIMA

ay isang daanan ng karera.

VROOM
BROOM!
1

6

S I X curves like a snail.

ANIM

ay kumukurba tulad ng suso.

A SNAIL! ISANG KUHOL!

7
SEVEN   has a sharp angle.
PITO
ay may matulis na anggulo.

OUCH!
ARAY!

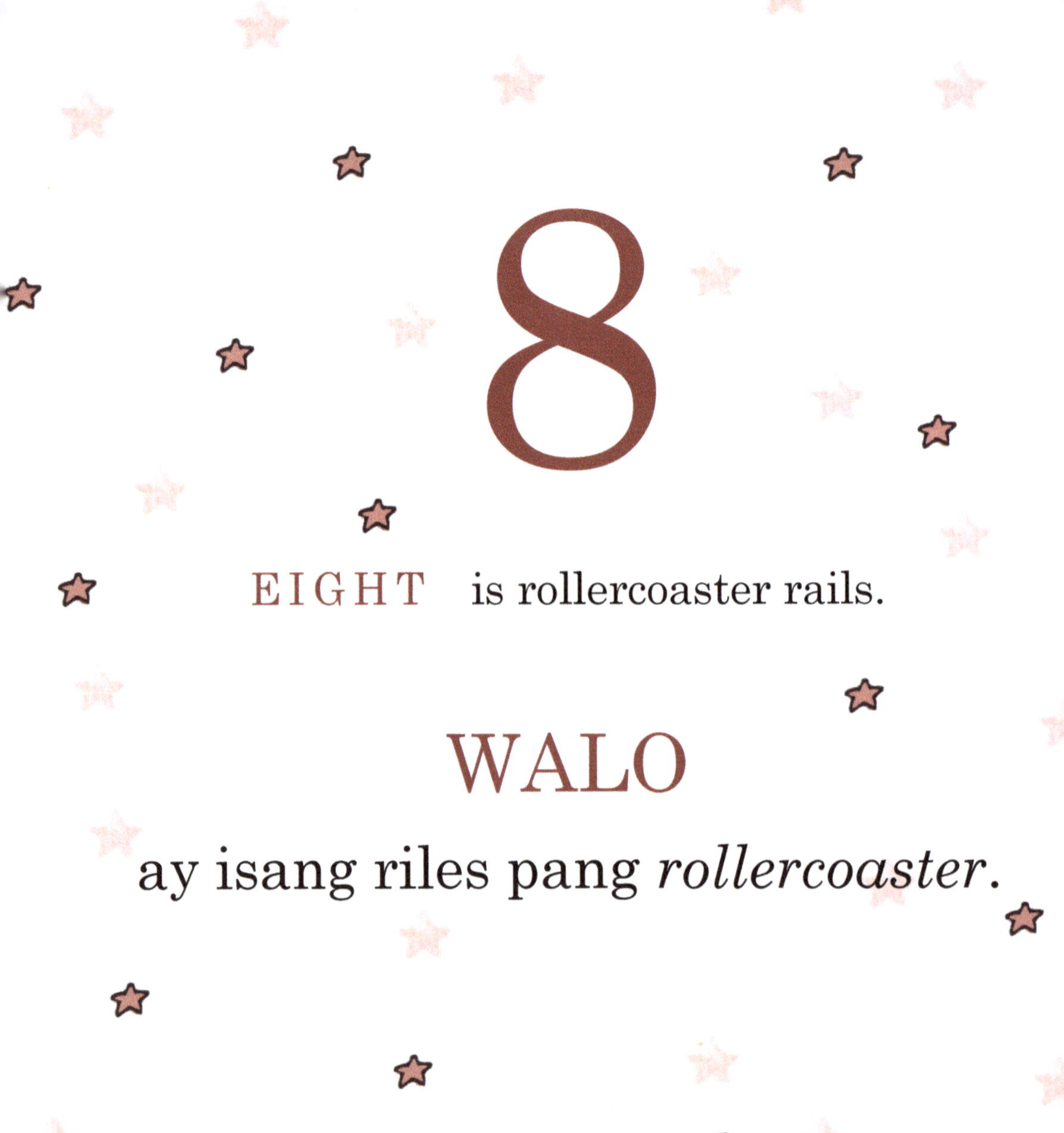

8

EIGHT   is rollercoaster rails.

WALO

ay isang riles pang *rollercoaster*.

YEHEY!
YIPPEE!

NINE   is a bubble on a stick.

SIYAM

ay isang bula sa patpat.

A BUBBLE! ISANG BULA!

10

TEN   is an eye of a whale.

SAMPU

ay isang mata ng balyena.

WINK!
KINDAT!
HELLO!   KAMUSTA!

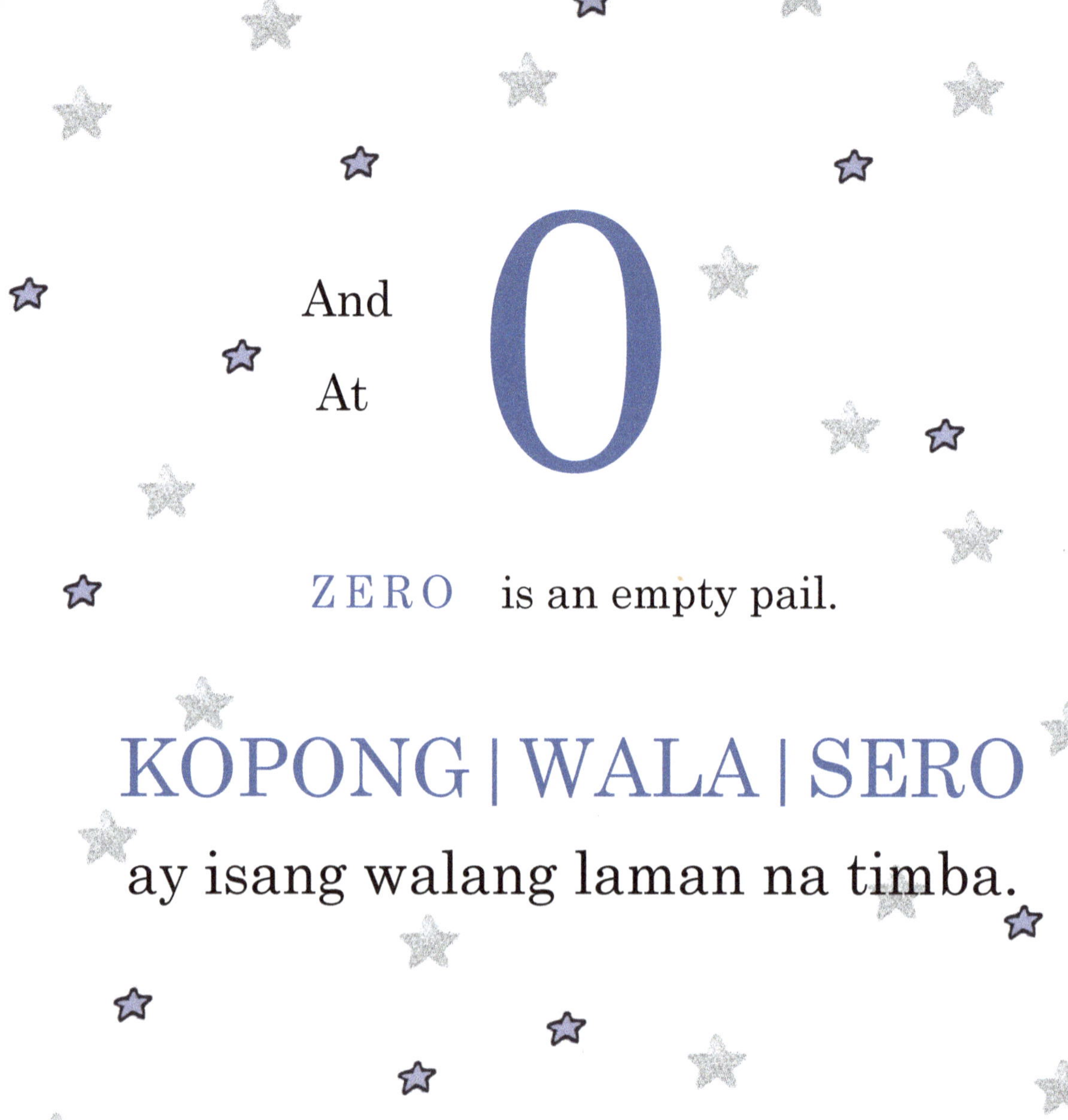
And
At

0

ZERO   is an empty pail.

KOPONG | WALA | SERO
ay isang walang laman na timba.

IT'S
EMPTY!
WALANG
LAMAN!

Thank you for playing with us today.

We had a lot of fun too!

Salamat sa pakikipaglaro sa amin ngayong araw.

Kami rin ay lubos na nasiyahan!

We are your Number friends,
Zero to Ten,
Who will be here for you~
Kami ang iyong mga kaibigan
Kopong hanggang Sampu.
Lagi kaming nandito para sa iyo.

Bye-bye now!
See you again soon.
Paalam sa ngayon!
Magkita tayong muli!

The Numbers are *SINGING* too!

To sing-a-long, look for Miss Anna Number Story
at your favorite music store like iTUNES.

MP3

Numbers 0-10
IDENTIFYING
& COUNTING

Numbers 11-20
& Ordinals
first, second, third...

Numbers 0-100
& Place Values
ones, tens, hundreds...

About Clocks
& Telling Time
hours, minutes, seconds

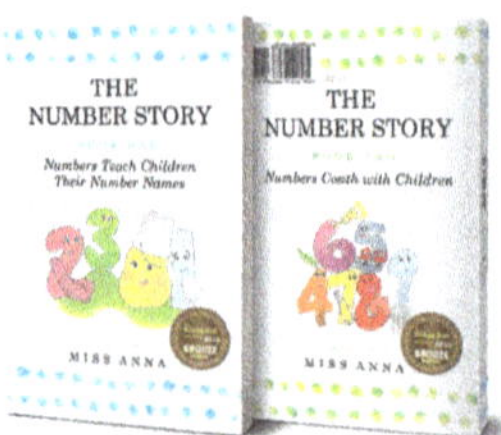

Number Story 1 & 2
isbn: 978-0-996216-48-7

Number Story 3 & 4
isbn: 978-1-945977-01-5

Number Story 5 & 6
isbn: 978-1-945977-06-0

Number Story 7 & 8
isbn: 978-1-949320-40-4

For more Miss Anna books to love,
visit us at

www.missannabooks.com

Numbers are working hard all over the world!
Come Travel the World with Us!

www.ingramcontent.com/pod-product-compliance
Lightning Source LLC
Chambersburg PA
CBHW041058050726

47599CB00018B/2198